大世界基尼斯

C·H·I·N·A R·E·C·O·R·D·S

纪录画册

互动版

上海大世界基尼斯总部 编

文匯出版社

编者的话

Editor's Note

这是一本奇妙的画册。

它的奇妙在于：读者可以通过手机或平板电脑下载“大世界基尼斯互动版”软件，让画册中平面图像在三维空间中活动起来，犹如魔幻小说中“魔法报纸”一样完整动态地展现图片中所含的全部景象，真切感受大世界基尼斯带来的惊奇和震憾。

它颠覆了传统纸质媒介的阅读特性，给予读者全新的体验，让阅读不再枯躁。

它实现了传统纸质媒介与现代科技的结合，运用新的形式展示大世界基尼斯的魅力，使大世界基尼斯更加精彩多姿。

这是一本励志的画册。

这里展现了能人奇士的智慧和勇气和超越自我，挑战极限的坚韧和刚毅，展示了草根英雄，勤劳勇敢，不惧困难，努力拼搏的自信和勇气，他们传递着我们社会的正能量，他们诠释了我们的民族精神。

这里承载了大世界基尼斯的光荣梦想，数十年的坚持和探索创新，只为打造具有中国特色、世界影响的民族品牌。扬民族之文化，激华夏之豪情，立中国之奇绝，创世界之新最是我们不断的追求。

《大世界基尼斯纪录画册》（互动版）浓缩了近历年来大世界基尼斯纪录的成果，讲述了一个个纪录创造者坚持奋斗的故事，图文并茂，动静结合，期望能给读者一个全新的体验感受，诚如一位哲人所说：只有不畏艰险奋勇登攀的人，才有希望到达光辉的顶点。

2013年9月

This is a wonderful picture album.

It is wonderful because readers can download "China Records Interactive Version" application to cell phone or tablet PC. It will make the flat images move in a 2D space. Just like the "magic newspaper" in magic fictions, it will dynamically present all images contained in the pictures and enable readers to feel the surprise and shock brought by China Records.

It overturns the reading character of traditional paper medium and provides readers with fresh and interesting experiences.

It integrates traditional paper medium and modern technologies and fully shows the charms and splendidness of China Records by using new forms.

This is an inspirational picture album.

It shows the wisdom, courage, determination, tenacity and fortitude of capable brains and talented people and depicts the industriousness, braveness and confidence of grass-roots heroes, who deliver positive energy of our society and interpret our national spirit.

It carries on the glorious dream of China Records. Having persisted in explorations and innovations for decades, we aim to create a national brand with Chinese characteristics and international influence. It is our eternal pursuit to carry forward national culture, to present the lofty sentiments of Chinese nation, to record the marvelousness of China and to set world records.

Record Picture Album of China Records (Interactive Version) condenses the results of China Records over the years and tells inspirational stories about many record makers with text and pictures. Through the association of activity and inertia, we expect to provide readers with brand new experiences and feelings. Just as a philosopher puts it, "only people with the courage to climb who are fearless of danger and difficulty may reach the peak of glory".

September 2013

编委名单：
Editors:

专家:
Experts:
侯 磊（法律） 吴少华（收藏）
Hou Lei(Law) · Wu Shaohua（Collect)
蒋昌忠（书画） 张顺龙（农艺）
Jiang Changzhong(Painting) · Zhang Shunlong(Agriculture)
陈学智（饮食） 陈金根（奇石）
Chen Xuezhi(Cooking) · Chen Jingen(Wonder Stone)
蒋国兴（陶艺） 毛东兴（声学）
Jiang Guoxing(Ceramic) · Mao Dongxing(Acoustics)
周曾同（医学） 杨守业（地质）
Zhou Zengtong(Medicine) · Yang Shouye(Geology)
周卫东（酒文化） 冯耀忠（微雕）
Zhou Weidong(Spirits Culture) · Feng Yaozhong(Microscopic Carvings)
刘一闻（书法篆刻） 汤兆基（工艺美术）
Liu Yiwen(Calligraphy & Seal Cutting) · Tang Zhaoji(Industrial Arts)
朱学稳（岩溶洞穴） 刘玉平（收藏·集邮）
Zhu Xuewen(Caverns) · Liu Yuping(Collecting Philately)
董枝明（古生物学） 崔文元（宝石鉴定）
Dong Zhiming(Paleontology) · Cui Wenyuan(Diamond & Jade Appraisal)
陈海波（瓷器） 余仰贤（陶瓷）
Chen Haibo(Porcelain) · Yu Yangxian(Ceramics)
周易杉（地质） 张阿根（地质）
Zhou Yishan(Geology) · Zhang Agen(Geology)
刘建军（林业） 汤崇贵（珠宝玉石·萤石球）
Liu Jianjun(Forestry) · Tang Chonggui（Gemstones · Fluorite Sphere）
韩男洙/韩国(民俗学)
Han Nam Su/Koren(Folklore)
满自喜日布扎赤·仁波切(佛学)
Manzushirbuza Trijang Rinpoche(Buddhism)

翻译、校对:
Translator、Proofreader:
上海世语翻译有限公司
Worldnese Translation Co.,Ltd.Shanghai

法律顾问:
Legal Adviser:
上海市锦天城律师事务所合伙人·邵鸣律师
All bright law officers · Shao Ming

我们的团队

扫描二维码下载软件

软件说明

1. 在手机或平板电脑中的APP STORE或安卓市场下载“大世界基尼斯互动版2013”软件。
2. 在画册中找到带有特殊记号的图片（该软件对画册之外的同张图片也具有相同识别功能）。
3. 打开软件，将摄像头对准图片，点击屏幕中出现的播放按钮（按钮可能出现在屏幕的任何位置，它只与实物相关，它的位置取决于实物在摄像头中的位置）。
   即可即时呈现您的精彩视频，感受'动'起来的世界!

目录
Contents

002号

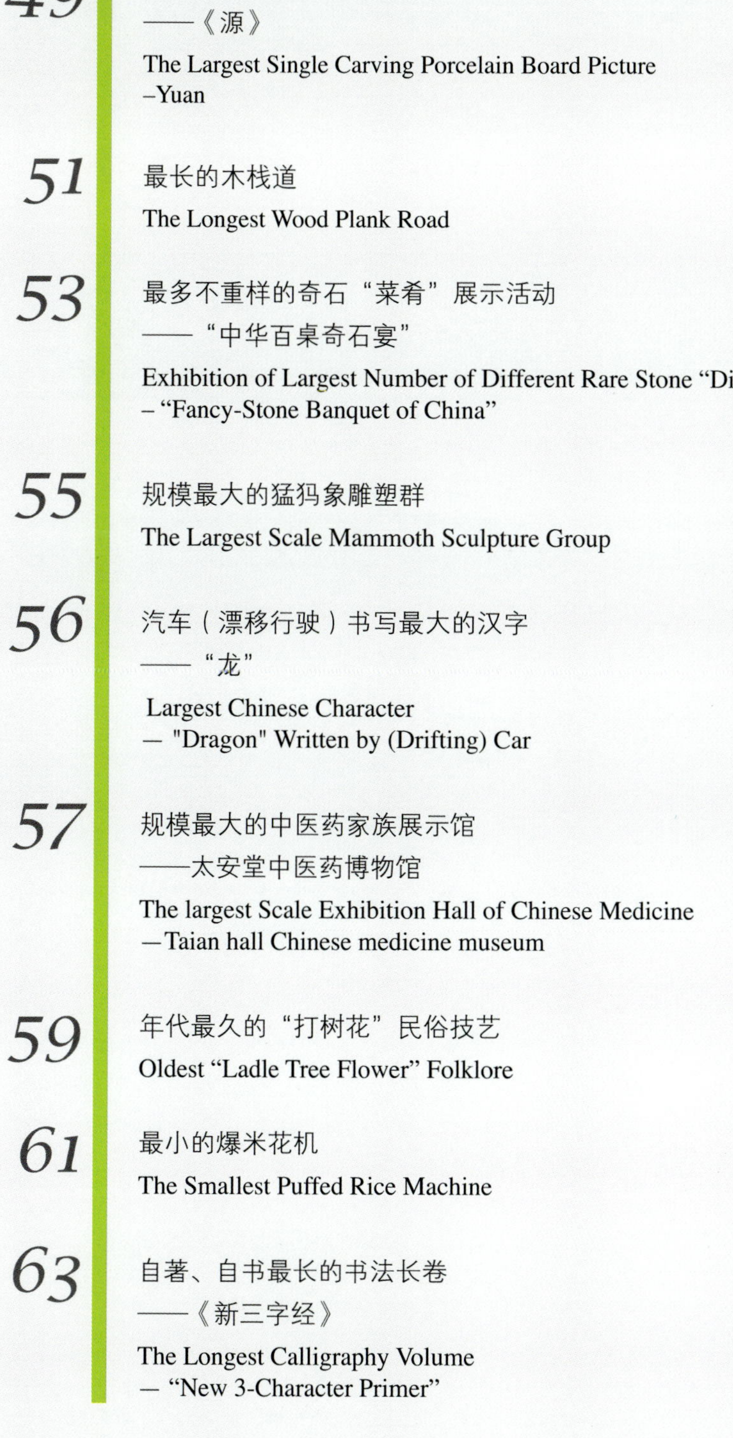

常州市教育局
常州创业精英商务俱乐部有限公司
汤友常文化展示中心

最大的戏楼（砖木结构）
——“草塘大戏楼”

The Largest Theatrical Stage (masonry-timber structure)
— “Caotang Theatrical Stage”

建筑面积：3773.6平方米
Building area: 3773.6m^2

该戏楼位于贵州省瓮安县草塘古邑区，占地面积1999.2平方米，选用83万余块大、小砖瓦及2468立方米巴西黄心木、南非红木、非洲巴帝木、香樟木等木材建造。

2013年8月1日竣工，贵州瓮安江界河国家级风景名胜区管理处管理。

This theatrical stage is located in Guyi district, Caotang, Wengan county, Guizhou province, which covers an area of 1999.2m^2. It is built up by using more than 830,000 pieces of big and small tiles and 2,468m^3 of Brazilian yellow heart wood, South African rosewood, African Bharti wood and camphor wood.

It was completed on August 1, 2013 and is managed by Jiangjie River national scenic area management office of Wengan, Guizhou.

最多城市同时举行的快闪活动

——“爱一夏，闪一下”

Across the Most Cities Were Held Simultaneously the Event —“Loving Flashing Summer”

2013年8月17日16时由中信银行股份有限公司信用卡中心主办，中信银行信用卡中心培训与发展中心承办的“爱一夏，闪一下 — 中信银行信用卡官方微信推广”快闪活动在深圳、北京、上海、广州等37个城市同时举行，共计4866人参加。

At 16 o'clock on August 17, 2013, Loving Flashing Summer, a marketing campaign to promote the official Wechat of CITIC credit card, organized by the Training and Development Center of CITIC Bank Credit Card Center who was the sponsor of the event, was carried out at the same time across 37 cities including Shenzhen, Beijing, Shanghai, Guangzhou and others, involving 4,866 participants.

数量：37
No. of cities: 37

张树成，艺名阿郎一笔（黑龙江·安达）2010年10月11日在河北沧州市狮城公园广场“第八届中国·沧州国际武术节”闭幕式现场，执2.01米硬笔在10×6米的布卷上一笔书写而成，用时19.09秒。

Zhang Shucheng, whose stage name is Alang Yibi (from Anda, Heilongjiang), wrote with a hard brush of 2.01m long in a cloth roll of 10×6m for 19.09 seconds at the closing ceremony of the “Eighth China International Martial Arts Festival • Cangzhou” held at Shicheng Park in Cangzhou City of Hebei Province on October 11, 2010.

现场书写**最大**的连笔空心字（单字）——“武”

Largest Single Stroke Outline Font Written on Site — a Chinese Character “武” (Wu)

尺寸：6×6 米
Size: 6 × 6m

最重的彩色石陨石

The Heaviest Colorful Meteoric Stone

该陨石（尺寸为54×53×37厘米）表面红绿相间并布满凹坑及小孔，发现于广西邕江河中。

中华赏石国学教育博物馆2008年10月收藏。

The surface of this meteorolite(size:54cm×53cm×37cm) is covered by red and green with pits and holes. It is discovered in the Yongjiang River in Guangxi province.

It was collected by the Chinese Stone Appreciation & National Culture Education Museum in October, 2008.

周国庆，浙江萧山人，现为中国观赏石协会副会长，浙江工商大学客座教授，中华赏石国学教育博物馆馆长。

最长的书法长卷

Longest Calligraphy Scroll

长：10363米
Length: 10,363m

周建松（江苏·江阴）2008年8月至2013年8月采用宣纸书写企业五十年发展大事记及《弟子规》、《三字经》、《道德经》、《唐诗、宋词三百首》、《四书五经》精要等装裱而成。

Zhou Jiansong (Jiangyin, Jiangsu Province) Written on Chinese art paper between August, 2008 and August, 2013 by Zhou Jiangsong, it contains the 50-year chronicle of events of the enterprise and the essentials of Di Zi Gui, Three-Character Classic, Tao Te King, 300 Tang Poems and 300 Song Lyrics, Four Books and Five Classics, etc., and is delicately framed.

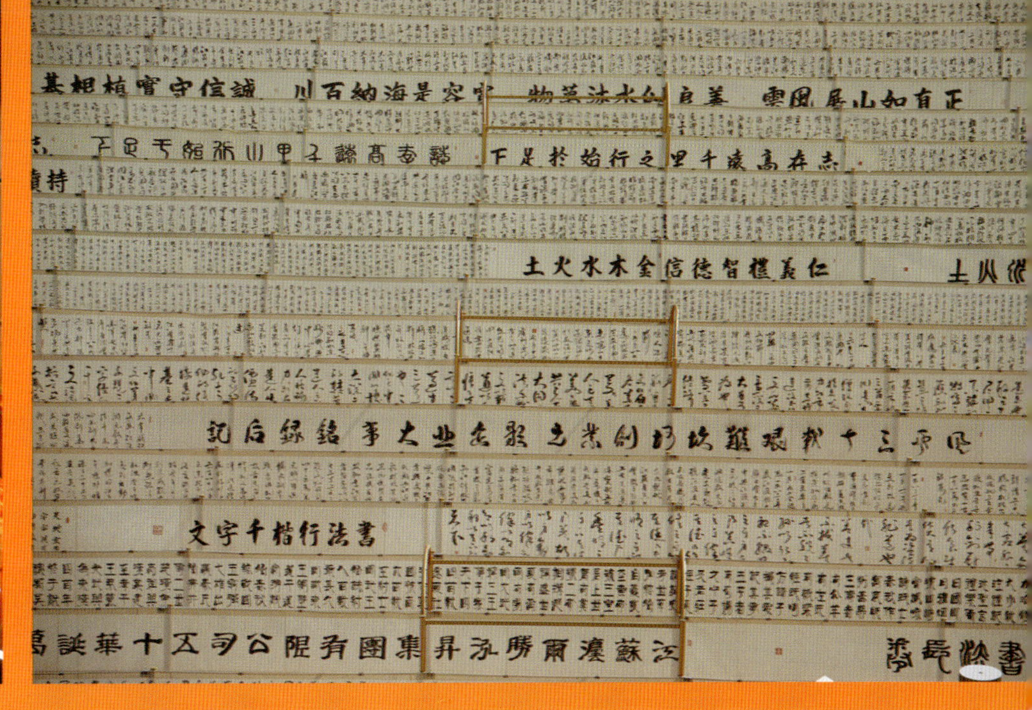

供奉缅甸白玉佛像最多的寺院
——“海南永庆寺”

“The Yongqing Temple of Hainan”
—The Temple with the Largest Number of White Jade Buddha Figures

佛像：42 尊
No. of Buddha Figures in the temple: 42

该寺院位于海南省澄迈县海南老城经济开发区盈滨半岛，寺内供奉释迦佛、卧佛、千手观音、文殊菩萨等佛像42尊，材质均为缅甸白玉。
（该项目荣获2010年第十二届大世界基尼斯最佳项目奖）

The temple is located in the Yingbin Peninsula, the Hainan Old City Economic Development zone of Chengmai County, Hainan Province. 42 Buddha Figures, all made of Burmese white jade, were consecrated in the temple, which include the figure of Sakyamuni(the Buddha), the Lying Buddha, the Thousand Hands Guanyin, and the Wenshu Bodhisattva.

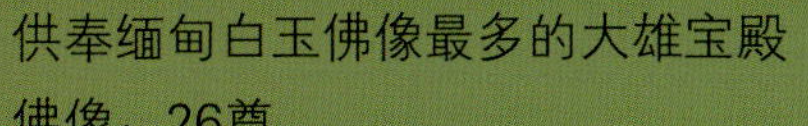

供奉缅甸白玉佛像最多的大雄宝殿

佛像：26尊

The Temple Propitiates Most of the Burma White Jade Buddha Statues

Number of Buddha statues: 26

最重的缅甸白玉阿弥陀佛

重：21.5吨

The heaviest Amitabha of Burma White

Weight: 21.5 tons

最高的缅甸白玉海岛观音

最高处：3.29米

The tallest Burma White Jade Sea Island Avalokitesvara statue

The highest elevation: 3.29m

最大的缅甸白玉弥勒佛

重：8.3吨

The biggest Burma White Jade Maitreya Buddha

Weight: 8.3 tons

同一题材自创诗、画、摄影作品最多的出版物

——《爱师竹篇》

The Publication with the Most Poems, Paintings, Photographical Works in the Same Subject Matter — Bamboo Loving

蒋昌忠（湖北·武汉）以竹为题创作的《爱师竹篇》诗·画·摄影集由湖北美术出版社2008年3月出版。

Bamboo Loving - Poem·Painting·Photographical Works was created by Jaing Changzhong (Wuhan Hubei) based on bamboos. The work was published by Hubei Art Press in March 2008.

诗、画、摄影：各 100

Number of works: 100 poems,
100 paintings, and 100 photographical works

字数最多的陶瓷微书作品

The Porcelain Tiny Handwriting with the Most Characters

字数：352963

书写面积6965.2平方厘米、平均值50.675字/平方厘米

Number of characters: 352963

Area of writing: 6965.2 square centimeters

Average area: 50.675 characters per square centimeters

王芝文（广东·汕头）1999年1月8日至2006年1月18日在33英寸陶瓷箭筒(高85厘米、直径29厘米)上书写《三国志》并经高温烧制而成。

Wang Zhiwen (Shantou. Guangdong) wrote The Romance of The Three Kingdoms on porcelain of 33 inches from January 8th 1999 to January 18th 2006. The art craft was made after being burned under high temperature.

三國志

规模最大的葵花园

——“百万葵园主题公园”

Largest Sunflower Garden

– “Million Sunflowers Subject Park”

数量：100 万株

占地面积：26 万平方米

Amount: one million　　Area: 260 thousand m²

“百万葵园”主题公园位于广州市番禺区新垦十五涌，全园种植的观赏性向日葵全部采用进口种子，由广州市葵花发展有限公司投资并于 2002年5月1日种植，4月26日正式对外开放观赏。

Invested by Guangzhou city sunflower development Ltd. Corporation, planted on May 1 2002 and opened to people on Apr 26, “Million Sunflowers” Subject Park lied in newly cultivated fifteen Yong Fanyu section Guangzhou city, and the seeds of sunflowers planted in the park for viewing and admiring were imported.

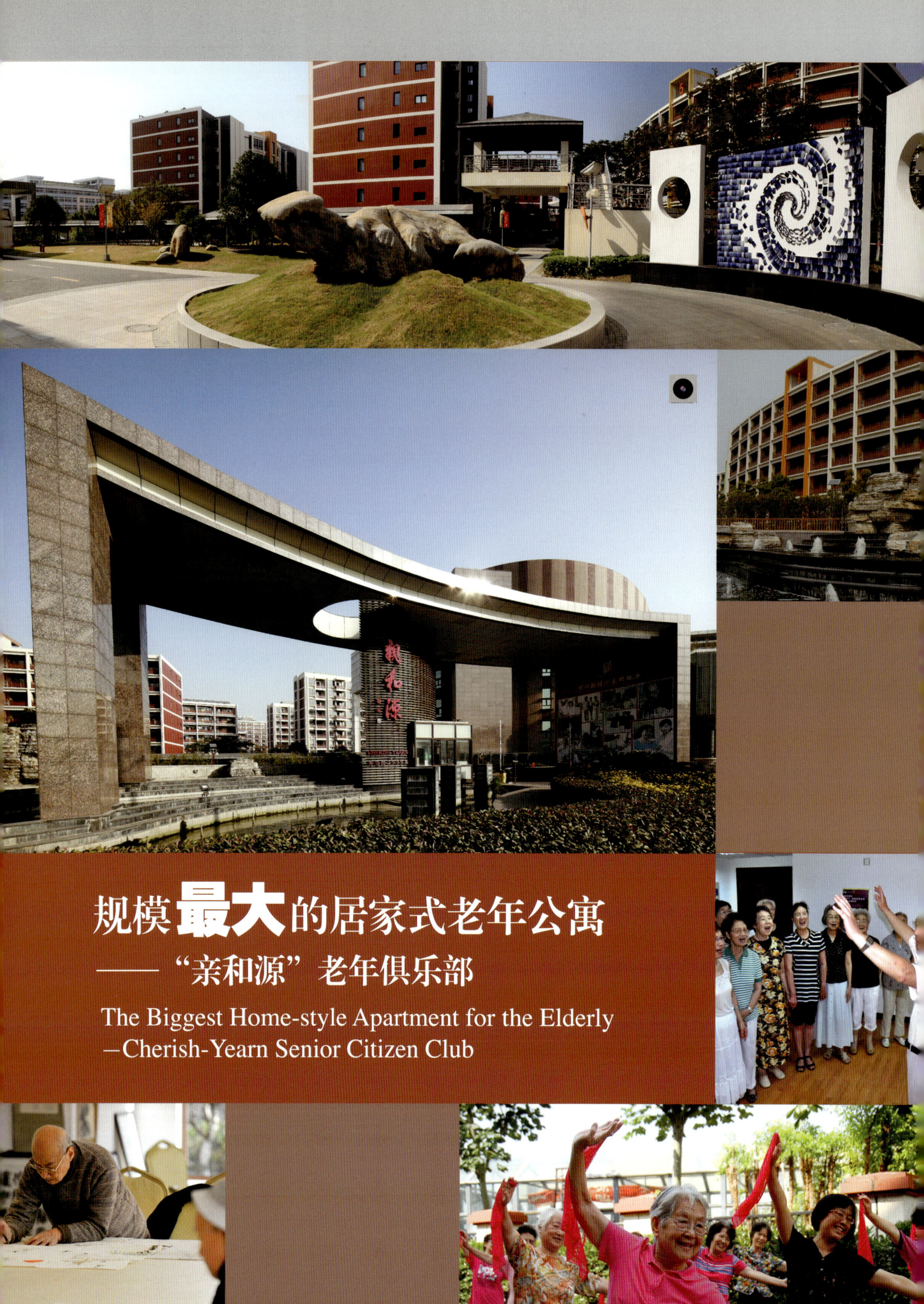

规模**最大**的居家式老年公寓

——“亲和源”老年俱乐部

The Biggest Home-style Apartment for the Elderly
–Cherish-Yearn Senior Citizen Club

套间：834
Suites: 834

“亲和源”位于上海市浦东新区康桥镇，占地83680平方米，总建筑面积近10万平方米，含老年公寓（分大、中、小户型共12栋）、会所、老年护理医院、配餐、管理、活动中心等16栋建筑。

2008年5月启用会员制模式运营，已有500余户老年家庭以户入住。

Cherish-Yearn lies in Kangqiao Town, Shanghai Pudong New Area, covering an area of 83,680 $m^2$with overall floorage of approaching 0.1 million m^2, including 16 buildings such as senior citizen apartments (a total of 12 big , middle, small houses), chambers, a nursing infirmary for the aged, catering, management and activity centers.

Membership model operation was initiated in May 2008, and over 500 aged families have moved in.

最大的银质鼻烟壶
——“那仁苏布德（太阳的珍珠）”

The Biggest Silver Snuff Bottle
— “Nelren Su Bude (pearl of the sun)

最高处: 92 厘米 最宽处: 81 厘米
Height: 92cm Width: 81cm

该鼻烟壶采用925银手工制作而成，壶身镶嵌271克珊瑚和80克天蓝色绿松石，并雕刻十二生肖图案，重20.5千克。
2011年由戴布仁（内蒙古·鄂尔多斯）收藏。

This snuff bottle was handcrafted out of 925 silver. The bottle body is inserted with 271-gram coral and 80-gram sky blue turquoise and is carved with the images of the twelve Chinese zodiac signs. The bottle weighs 20.5kg.
It was collected by Dai Buren (Inner Mongolia·Erdos) in 2011.

最多幅自书画笺书法作品（个人）展

——“中国第一榜书”作品展

The Calligraphy(personal) Exhibition with the Maximum Number of Piece of Paintings

— The “Best Calligraphy of China” Exhibition

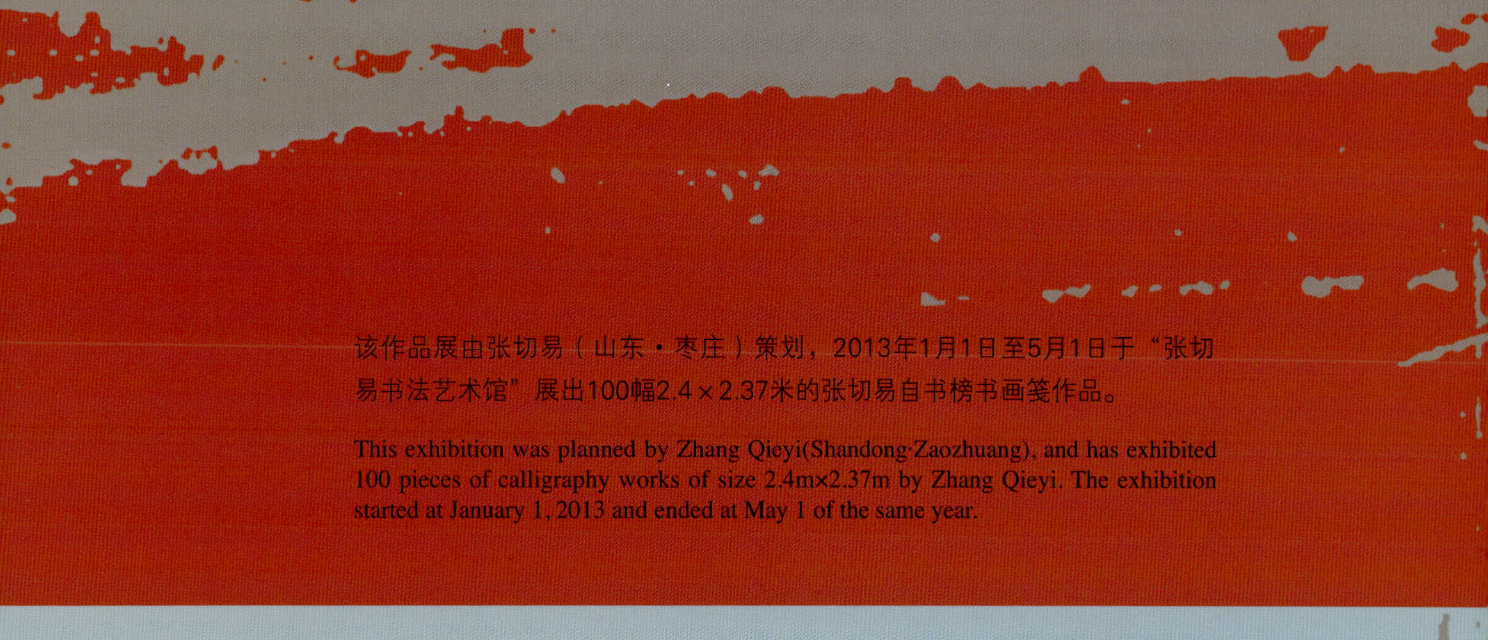

该作品展由张切易（山东·枣庄）策划，2013年1月1日至5月1日于“张切易书法艺术馆”展出100幅2.4×2.37米的张切易自书榜书画笺作品。

This exhibition was planned by Zhang Qieyi(Shandong·Zaozhuang), and has exhibited 100 pieces of calligraphy works of size 2.4m×2.37m by Zhang Qieyi. The exhibition started at January 1, 2013 and ended at May 1 of the same year.

数量：100 幅

Quantity: 100 pieces

规定时间内空竹3米对抛次数之最

The Largest Number of Times of Throwing a Diabolo Toward and Receiving One From Each other Within a Specified Time

时间：60 秒
次数：87 次
Time: 60s; times: 87

钱波、钱涛（浙江·绍兴）60秒内分别将空竹抛向对方，并接住对方抛来的空竹87次。2013年5月21日在绍兴市快阁苑小学多功能室创造。

Qianbo and Qiantao (Shaoxing, Zhejiang Province) respectively threw a diabolo toward and received one from each other, and the process was repeated for 87 times within 60s. Realized in the multi-function room of Kuaigeyuan Primary School on May, 21, 2013.

最长的长板鞋（拼接）竞走活动

The Longest Board Shoes (Splicing) Walking Race

板鞋长：50.21米
Length of Board Shoes: 50.21 M

2010年7月26日在广西南宁市人民会堂前小广场，由广西群众艺术馆组织108名选手在23对板鞋拼接而成的长板鞋上创造，竞走距离31.95米。

108 competitors participated in the walking race organized by Guangxi Mass Art Center at the small square in front of the People's Hall in Nanning City of Guangxi Province on July 26, 2010. The record was created by a walking race on a long board shoe, spliced by 23 pairs of board shoes, with walking distance of 31.95 meters.

许洪（福建·诏安）1999年8月至2003年3月自创110首以旅游为主题的诗词，并亲笔书写、镌刻于石板上。

From August 1999 to March 2003, Xu Hong (Zhao'an, Fujian) created 110 tourism-themed poems and personally wrote and engraved them on stone tablets.

书写自创诗词并镌刻诗碑数量之最

——“许洪百首诗碑”

“Xu Hong's Hundred Poem Table” – Writing and Engraving Most Original Poems on Poem Tablets

数量：100 块

Number: 100 Tablets

西禅古寺建何年

游西禅寺

共和庚辰年季许 洪祥書

鍾門巨浪

峯頂撫蒼穹 果然青葱 虬松盤踞绿林中 槐柳藤蘿迷古道 领盡秋風 巨浪拍朦朧 瞬息無踪 遥聆雁陣列長空 往事烟消殘勒石 氣吐如虹

浪淘沙 悬鍾果老山

共和辛巳年深秋 许洪祥书

羅星塔上攬星星

馬江祭

郡王鞭指正紅東

鄭成功

手抄**最多**部国学作品的出版物

——《李土生手抄国学经典》

The Publication with the Most Handwriting Sinology works
– LiTusheng's Handwriting Sinology Classic

数量：70
书号：ISBN 978-7-5073-3395-4
Quantity: 70
Book number: ISBN 978-7-5073-3395-4

该作品收录李土生（浙江·东阳）抄写的《大学》、《中庸》、《论语》、《弟子规》、《心经》、《大悲咒》等70部国学作品，计36万字。2011年10月由中央文献出版社出版，印刷装订为四函二十册。

This work has collected 70 pieces of works that were handwritten by Li Tusheng(Zhejiang·Dongyang), including "The Great Learning", "Doctrine of the Mean", "Analects of Confucius", "Disciples Regulation", "Heart Sutra" and "Great Compassion Mantra" with total characters of about 360,000.
It was published by the Central Literature Publishing House and was bound into four cases of 20 copies in October, 2011.

大块假我以文章

刘大为画集
Liu Dawei Arts

天堆佔德

2011年8月6日由中共新宁县委、新宁县人民政府主办、崀山风景名胜区管理处承办、长沙御峰体育文化有限公司执行的“通天壮举 崀山见证—赛买提·艾山2011崀山高空热气球走钢丝”活动在湖南省崀山辣椒峰景区举行，赛买提·艾山（新疆·乌鲁木齐）在两只漂浮的热气球间架设的钢丝上行走完成。

On August 6, 2011, the ‘Heroic Event in Mount Lang—2011 High-wire Walking over Hot Air Balloon by Saimaiti Aishan (from Urumchi in Xinjiang Uygur Autonomous Region)’ activity, hosted by CPC Xinning County Party Committee and Xinning County People’s Government, undertaken by Mount Lang Scenic Area Management Office and executed by Changsha Yufeng Sports Culture Co., Ltd, was held in Lajiao Peak scenic area of Mount Lang in Hunan Province. In this event, Saimaiti Aishan completed walking on the high-wire suspended by hot air balloons.

在两只漂浮的热气球间走钢丝距离之最

Longest High-wire Walking Between Two Floating Hot Air Balloons

钢丝长：15 米　离地高：30 米

时间：3 分 38 秒

Wire length: 15m, height from ground: 30m

Time: 3 minutes 38 seconds

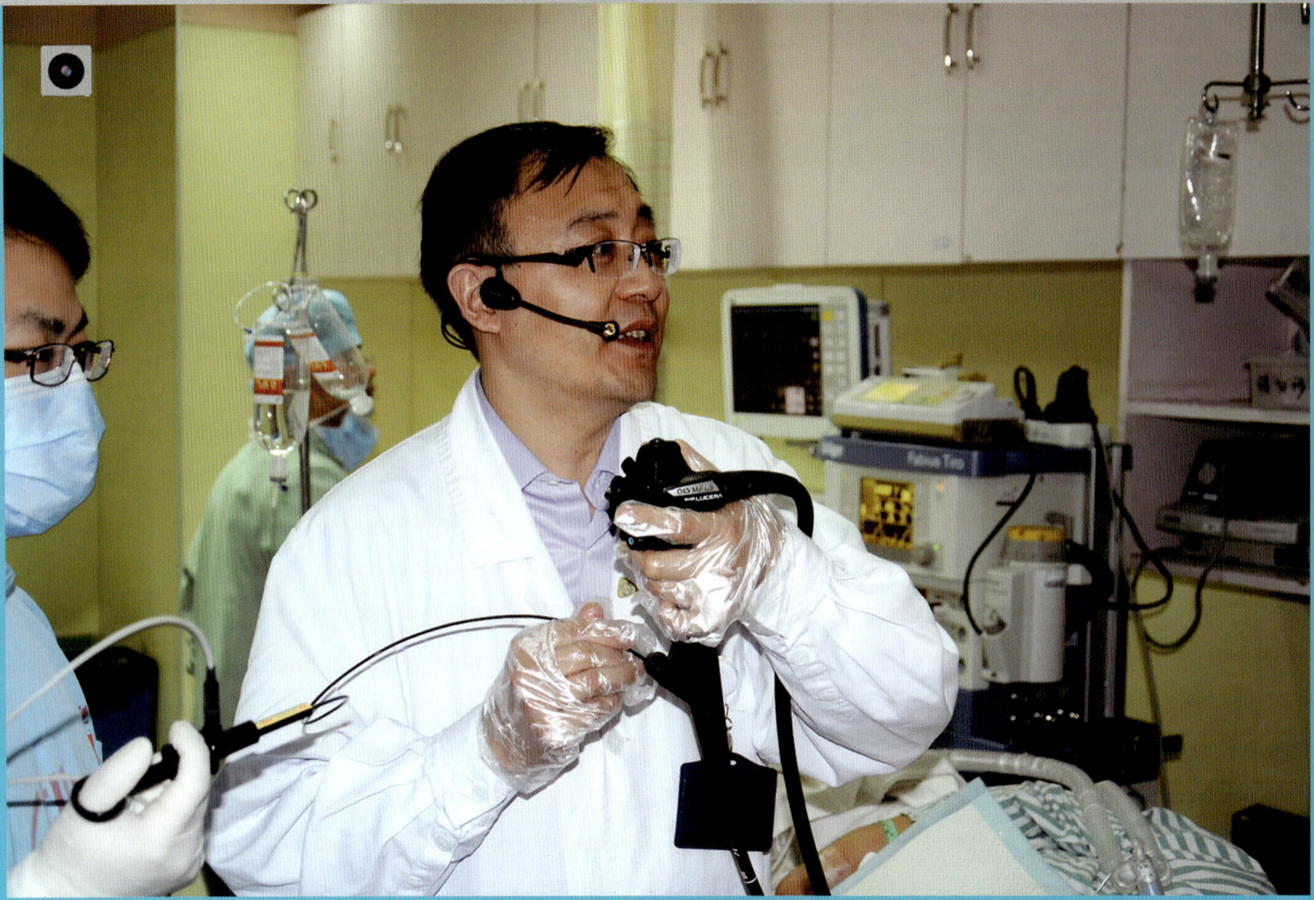

通过胃镜手术切除的**最大**脂肪瘤

The Largest Lipoma Removed by Gastrostomy

2013年2月21日复旦大学附属中山医院内镜中心周平红（上海）教授通过胃镜手术，使用海博刀为患者切除并从口中取出重124克的食管脂肪瘤。

On February, 21, 2013, Zhou Pinghong (Shanghai), a professor working at the Endoscopy Center of Zhongshan Hospital affiliated to Fudan University, removed from the patient's esophagus a lipoma weighing 124g with Hybrid Knife by gastrostomy.

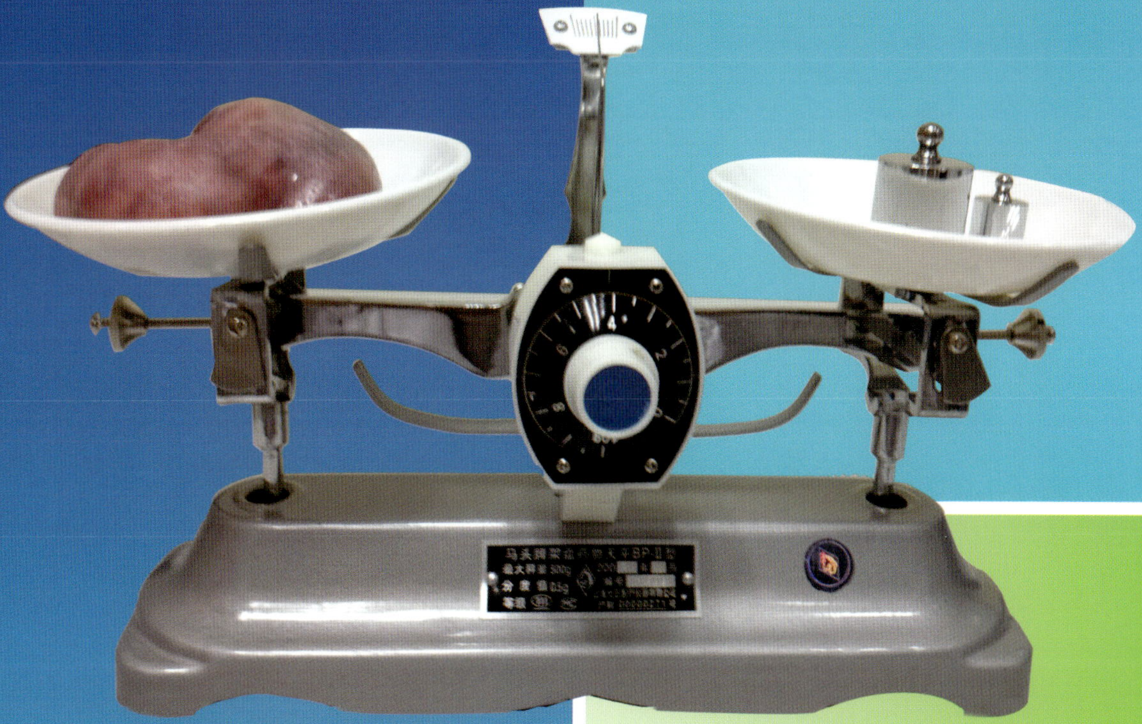

尺寸：**16×5.5×4** 厘米

Size: 16 × 5.5 × 4cm

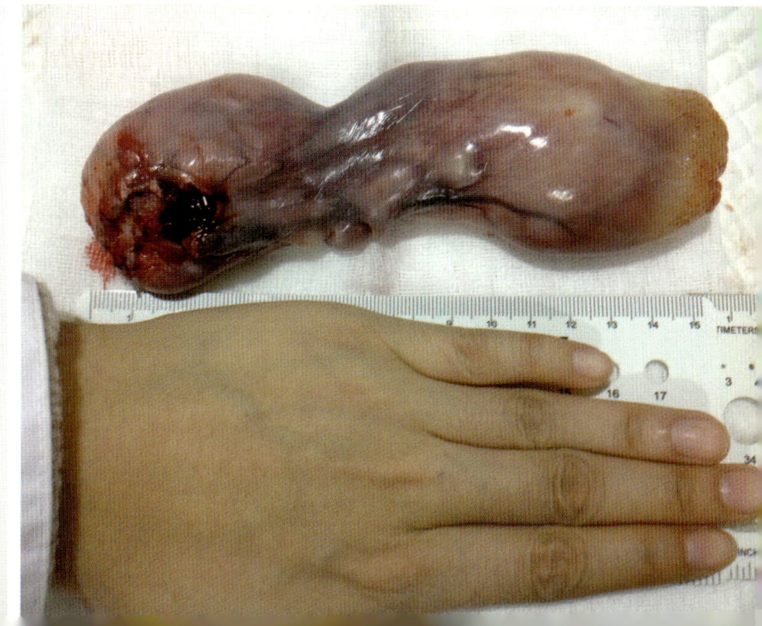

最小的中国画
——《清明上河图》

The Smallest-sized Chinese Painting
— Riverside Scene at Qingming Festival

长：84 厘米　宽：4 厘米
Length: 84cm　Width: 4cm

吴梅初（上海）1988年6月10日至1990年1月5日根据《清明上河图》原作全景微画在宣纸上，其中人物850余人（最大的高0.5厘米、最小的0.3厘米）；动物、牲畜50多头；大小船只20多条及车、桥等。

Produced by Wu Meichu (Shanghai) from June 10 1988 to January 1, 1990. It dwindles the panorama of the famous picture Qingming Upstream Picture on the rice paper, including 850 characters (the biggest is 0.5cm, the smallest is 0.3cm),50 animals and livestock and more than 20 boats and several vehicles or bridges etc.

最大的萤石球

Largest Fluorite Ball

该萤石球呈圆球状，表面黄绿色覆保护膜。
浙江省武义县武阳春雷工艺品厂2001年6月收藏。

The fluorite ball is of spherical shape, with yellowish green surface covered with protective film.
The ball was collected in June, 2001 by Wuyang Chunlei Art and Craft Plant in Wuyi County, Zhejiang Province.

直径：**175**厘米 重：**8.53**吨 折射率：**1.42**

Diameter: 175cm, weight: 8.53ton

Refractive index: 1.42

最多 亲子参加的绘画捐书活动

The Painting and Book Donating Activity with the Largest Number of Parents and Children Participated

2013年4月20日至2013年5月26日，由江苏中基置业发展有限公司主办，香港文汇报上海分社承办的“天成佳园幸福无处不在——100天大世界基尼斯纪录置换希望小学图书馆计划”公益活动中，来自昆山市柏庐小学、昆山经济开发区中华园小学、昆山三之三幼儿园、昆山大德世家幼儿园、昆山新城域幼儿园的1253对亲子在999米画轴上绘画并捐赠书籍。

From April, 20, 2013 to May, 26, 2013, the “Happiness is Everywhere in Tianchengjiayuan- Plan of Library Replacement for Hope Primary Schools Creating a Great World Guinness Record in 100 Days” activity was hosted by Jiangsu Zhongji Property Development Co., Ltd. and organized by Shanghai Branch of Hong Kong Wenwei News, and 1,253 pairs of parents/children from Kunshan Bolu Primary School, Zhonghuayuan Primary School of Kunshan Economic & Technological Development Zone, Kunshan Sanzhisan Kindergarten, Kunshan Dadeshijia Kindergarten and Kunshan Xincheng Kindergarten painted on the 999m-long scroll and donated their books.

亲子数量:1253

Number of pairs: 1,253

连续转呼啦圈数量之最

The Record of Simultaneously Rolling Hula Hoops

数量：300 只

No. of Hula Hoops Rolled: 300

金琳琳（黑龙江·哈尔滨）同时转起300个呼啦圈，持续24秒。

2009年3月29日在日本NTV国家电视台录制的《冲击2009》节目中创造。

Jin Linlin (Harbin Heilongjiang Province) simultaneously rolled a total of 300 hula hoops for a time of 24 seconds. This record was made during the Impact 2009, a program recorded by Japan National TV Station on Mar 29, 2009.

最长距离的溜冰过杆

Passing the Horizontally-Set Poles by Skating in the Longest Distance

横杆：平均高0.232米、宽1.972米；数量47根、间距1米

李明芬（广东·佛山）2006年11月13日在佛山市顺德区新城区德胜广场创造。

Average height of the poles from the ground: 0.232m Width: 1.972m

Nimber: 47 poles Distance between every two poles: 1m

Created by Li Mingfen (Foshan Guangdong) at Desheng Square Xincheng Shunde District Foshan City on November 13th 2006.

距离：46.101 米

Distance: 46.101m

最高的水上景观雕塑
——“中国结”

Tallest Water Landscape Sculpture
–“Chinese Knot”

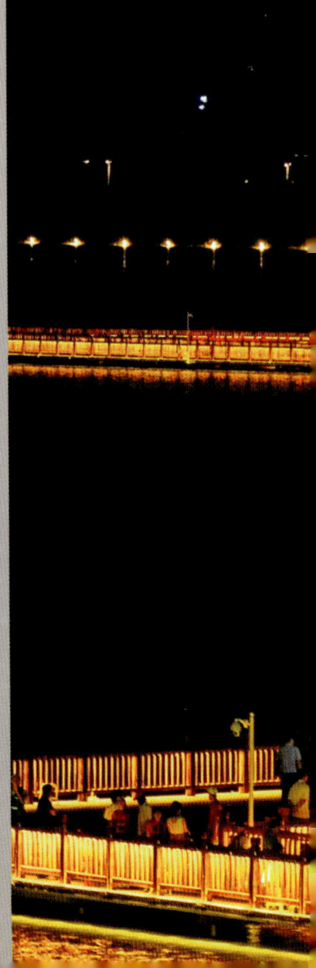

该雕塑以“中国结”为原型，用塔式钢结构建造，2013年7月竣工，现矗立于大庆市龙凤区三永湖之上。

黑龙江省大庆市城市管理委员会管理。

Taking “Chinese knot” as its prototype, the sculpture adopts a tower-type steel structure. Completed in July 2013, it now stands over Sanyong Lake, Longfeng District, Daqing City.

Managed by Urban Management Committee, Daqing City, Heilongjiang Province

最大的丝棉画

The Largest Silk Cotton Painting

长：10.36米 宽：4米
Length: 10.36m width: 4m

袁洪滨（安徽·马鞍山）设计的《千古一秀采石矶》选用上乘丝棉材料，经高温、高压、染色和手工技艺，2007年12月至2008年5月20日制作完成。

该作品现展示于安徽省马鞍山市会议中心第一接待厅。

The painting The Quarry, An Outstanding Beauty was designed by Yuan Hongbing (Ma'anshan Anhui) with qualified silk cotton. The work underwent high temperature, high pressure, dying and handwork techniques. It was made from Decmber 2007 to May 20th 2008 and displayed in No.1 Reception Hall of Ma'anshan City Conference Center, Anhui Province.

最大的独幅雕刻瓷板画

——《源》

The Largest Single Carving Porcelain Board Picture–Yuan

长：3.36 米　宽：1.56 米

Length: 3.36m　Width: 1.56m

许爱民（江西·黎川）设计、创作，2007年3月1日至7月26日在以手工制成的瓷泥坯板（厚8至9毫米）上雕刻图案和施釉，经1360度高温烧制、彩绘后再经过760度烤花而成。

Xu Aimin (Lichuan Jiangxi) designed and created this work. From March 1st to July 26th 2007 he carved pictures and applied glaze on a piece of hand-made porcelain base which was 8mm to 9mm thick. Then he burnt the base in the high temperature of 1360 degrees and colored the drawing. Finally he gave the work decorating firing in 760 degrees.

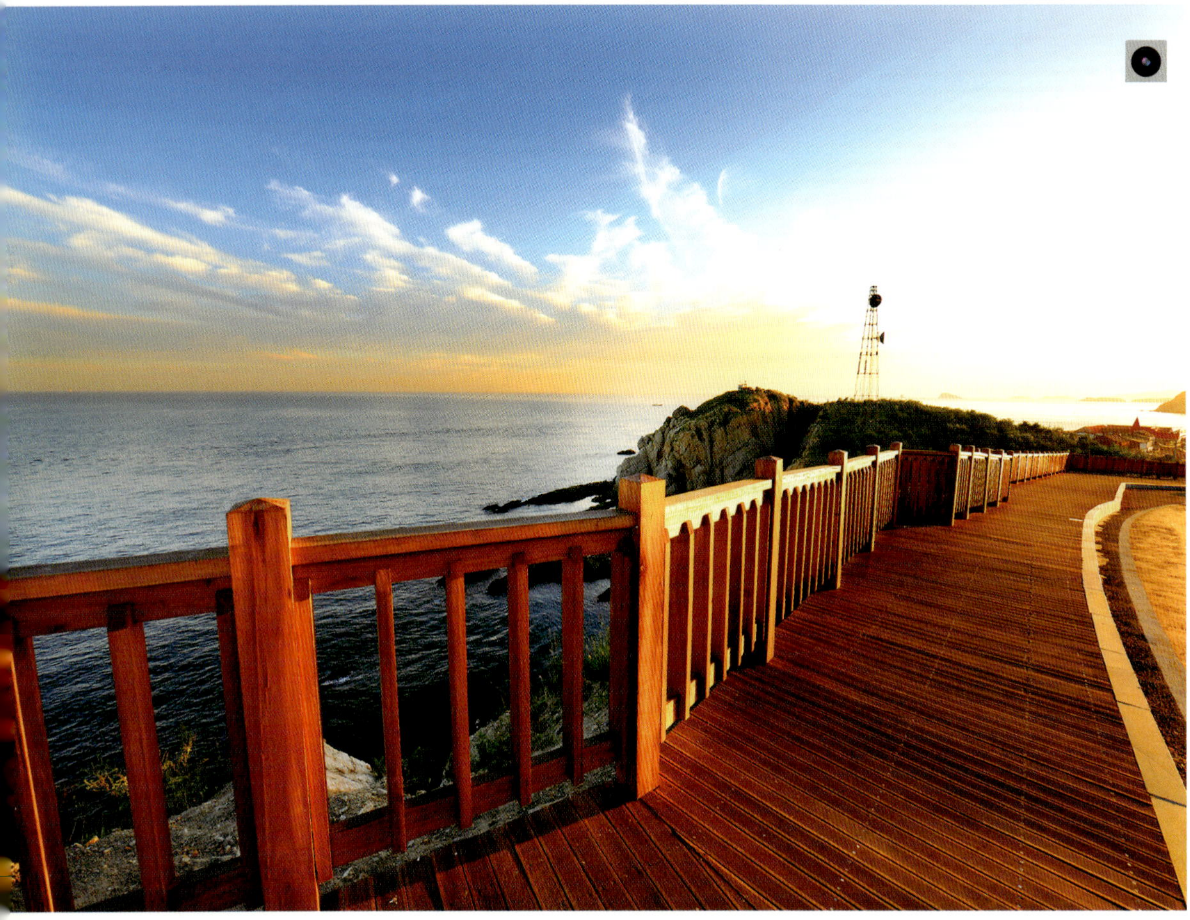

最长的木栈道

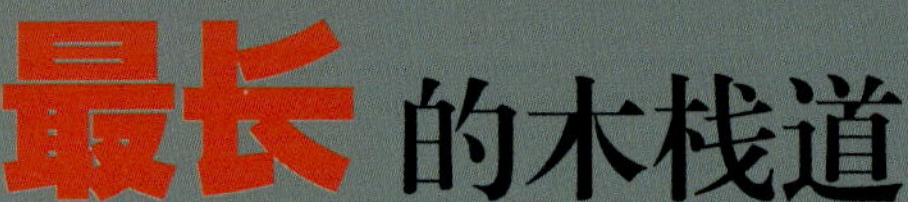

The Longest Wood Plank Road

长：20.99千米
Length: 20.99 km

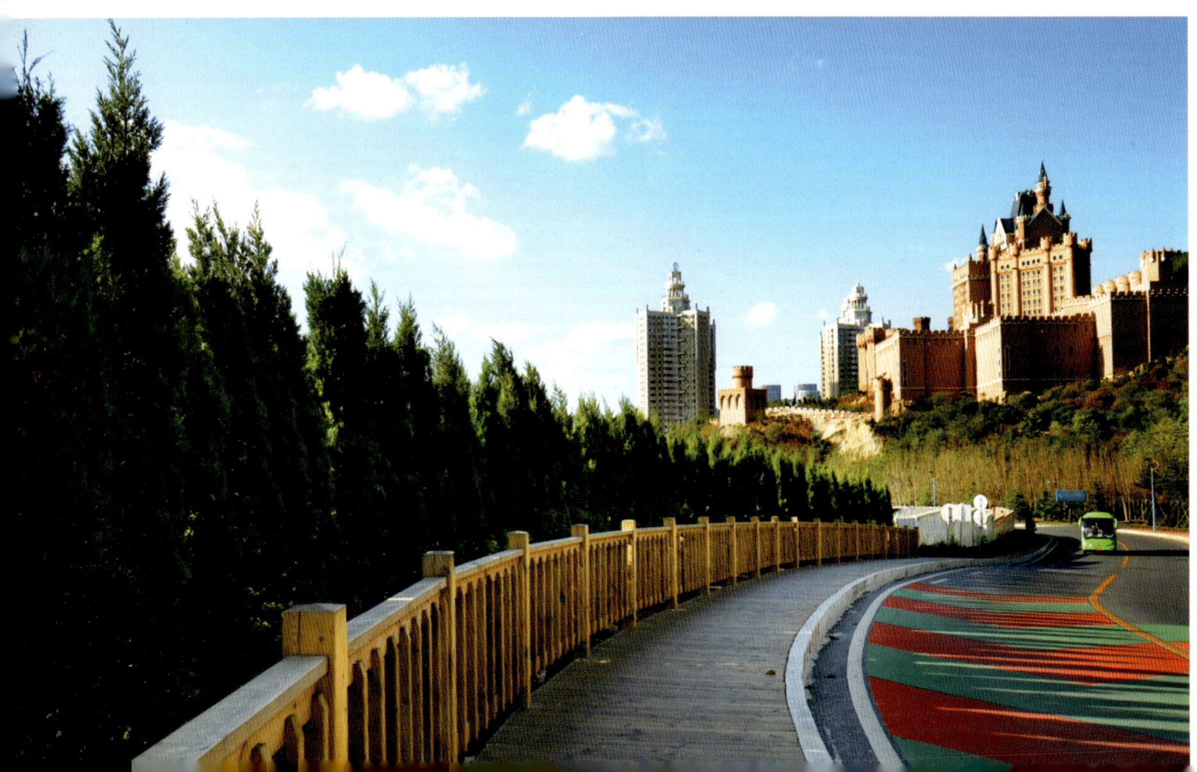

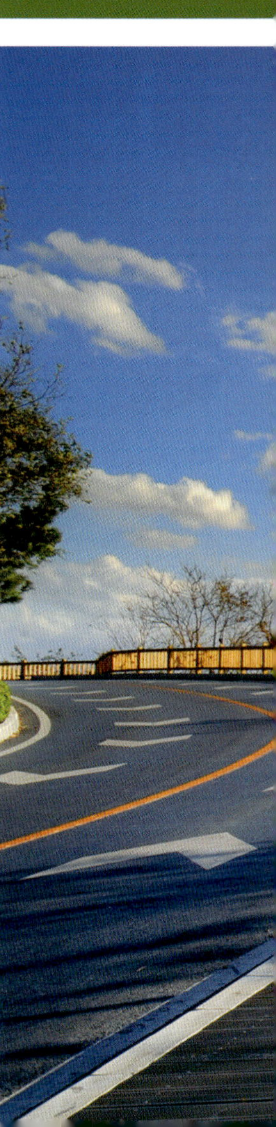

由大连市人民政府投资建设的大连滨海路人行木栈道采用俄罗斯樟子松和南美巨桉木建成。起自星海湾大桥，止于海之韵公园，最宽处17.18米，最窄处0.85米，沿途设11个观景台，修建落差68米。2008年5月24日开工建设，2009年8月28日竣工。

The wood plank road that built along the Dalian Binhai road was invested by the People's Government of Dalian Municipality and constructed with Pinus Sylvestris wood from Russia and Eucalyptus wood from Latin America. It starts from Xinhaiwan Bridge and wriggled unill the Sea Charm Park. The widest stretch is 17.18m, and the narrowest section is only 0.85m. There are 11 Observation Decks along the road with a 68m drop height. The project is commenced on May 24, 2008 and completed on August 28, 2009.

最多不重样的奇石“菜肴”展示活动
——“中华百桌奇石宴”

Exhibition of Largest Number of Different Rare Stone “Dishes” – “Fancy-Stone Banquet of China”

数量：6392 道
Number: 6,392 “Courses”

2013年9月29日在由内蒙古阿拉善方一漠玉淘宝城主办的“中华百桌奇石宴”展览会上，参展方将奇石组成“烤全羊”、“东坡肘”、八宝粥”、“红烧肉”等不重样的6392道川、鲁、湘、粤“菜肴”及“满汉全席”，共105桌。

On September 29, 2013, sponsored by Fang Yi Desert Jade Taobao Shopping City, Alxa, Inner Mongolia, “Fancy-Stone Banquet of China” exhibited totally 105 tables and 6,392 courses of Sichuan, Shandong, Hunan and Guangdong dishes, including Roast Whole Lamb, Dongpo Braised Elbow, Mixed Congee, Stewed Pork with Brown Sauce, etc.

猛獁故鄉

一 扎賚諾爾

规模最大的猛犸象雕塑群

The Largest Scale Mammoth Sculpture Group

该雕塑群落占地7.9万平方米，位于内蒙古呼伦贝尔市扎赉诺尔区猛犸公园内，其中单体象王高15.77米、长15.9米、宽4.4米。

2012年5月至2013年6月建成,内蒙古满洲里市扎赉诺尔区猛犸公园管理处管理。

This sculpture group covers an area of 79,000 m^2 and is located in the Jalainur Mommoth park in Hulunbuir city of Inner Mongonia. And the mammoth king is as high as 15.77m, as long as 15.9m and as wide as 4.4m.

It was built up from May, 2012 to June, 2013 and is now under the management of the Administrative Office of the Jalainur Mommoth park in Manchuria city of Inner Mongonia.

数量：87 座

quantity: 87

汽车（漂移行驶）书写最大的汉字——“龙”

Largest Chinese Character — "Dragon" Written by (Drifting) Car

长：74 米　宽：57 米　用时：42 秒
Length: 74m　Width: 57m
Time Consumption: 42 seconds

2013年3月13日（农历二月初二）由河南省濮阳市人民政府、市委宣传部、市文化广电新闻出版局、市体育局、濮阳龙文化产业发展促进会联合举办的“2013濮阳‘二月二’龙文化体育系列活动之汽车书龙”中，桑文军（河南·濮阳）驾驶配置特殊装置的轿车在市文化艺术中心广场用漂移轨迹“书写”唐代书法家张旭的草书“龙”。

On March 13th, 2013 (February 2nd in lunar calendar), in "2013 Puyang 'February 2nd Spring Dragon Festival' Dragon Culture Sports Activities – Car Writing Dragon" jointly held by Henan Puyang Municipal People's Government, Municipal Propaganda Department, Municipal Department of Culture, Radio, Film, TV, Press and Publication, Municipal Bureau of Sports, Puyang Dragon Culture Industrial Development Promotion Association, Sang Wenjun (Puyang, Henan) drove the car equipped with special device to "write" the character of "Dragon" in the cursive script of Zhang Xu (calligrapher in Tang Dynasty) with the car drifting traces in the Municipal Central Plaza of Culture and Art.

规模最大的中医药家族展示馆

——太安堂中医药博物馆

The largest Scale Exhibition Hall of Chinese Medicine
—Taian hall Chinese medicine museum

建筑面积：3200 平方米
The Architecture Area: 3,200m^2

"太安堂"源于1567年，现由第十三代传人柯树泉经营管理，系家族制药企业。太安堂中医药博物馆共两层，位于汕头市金园工业区新建太安堂制药厂区内，以潮州柯氏十三代中医药世家的历史渊源和太安堂发展轨迹作为情节线索，展示了太安堂深厚中医药文化底蕴的重要物品，如珍贵医书、明清时期的诊疗器具、锦旗、牌匾等。

"Tanan hall" was established in1567 and it was family enterprise of pharmacy and managed by Ke Shuquan who is thirteenth generation. There are 2 floors in the new building of Taian hall that located at Shantou gold garden industrial district drugs manufacture factory.

年代最久的“打树花”民俗技艺

Oldest "Ladle Tree Flower" Folklore

年数：约 530 年

Age: about 530 years

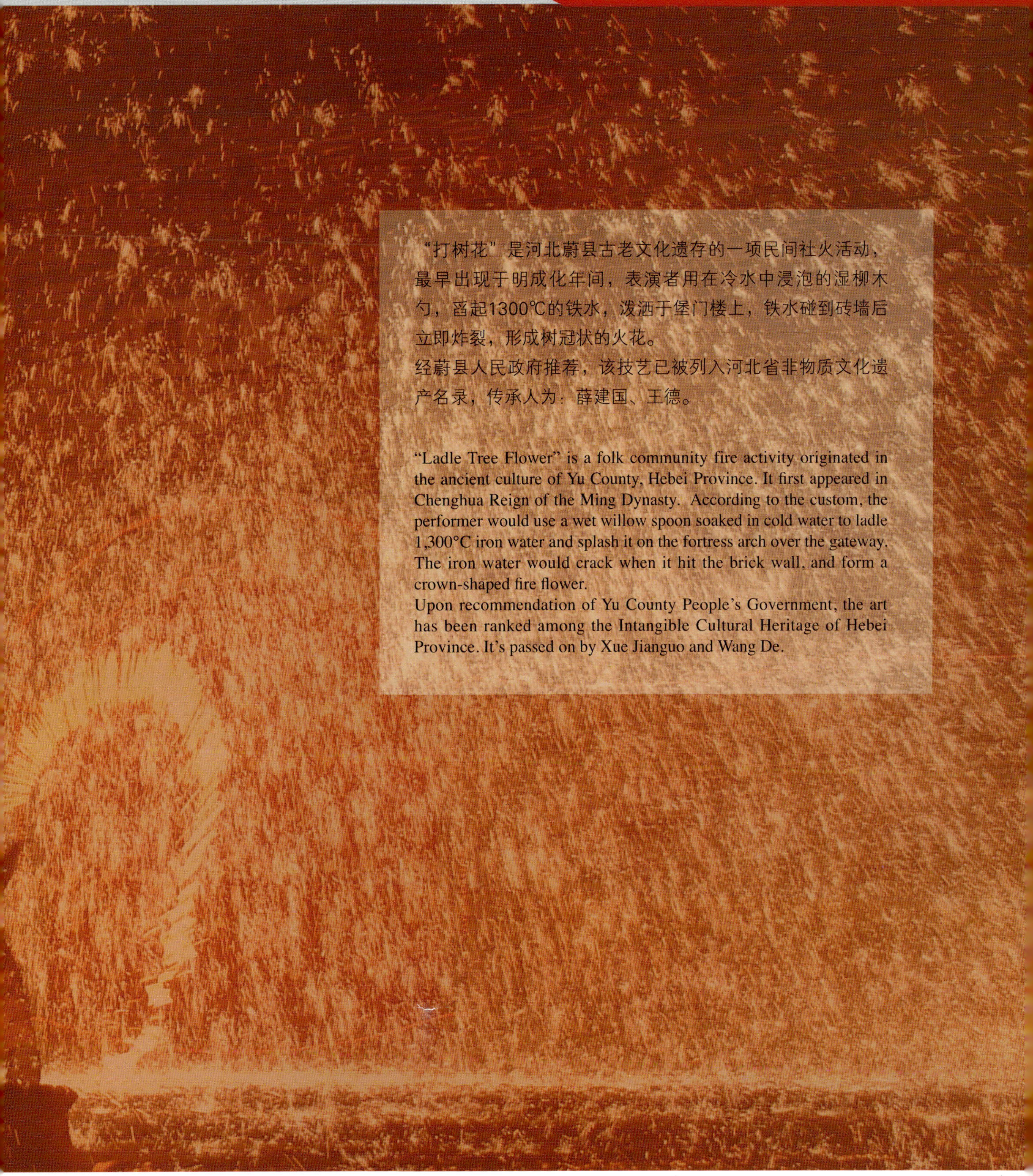

“打树花”是河北蔚县古老文化遗存的一项民间社火活动，最早出现于明成化年间，表演者用在冷水中浸泡的湿柳木勺，舀起1300℃的铁水，泼洒于堡门楼上，铁水碰到砖墙后立即炸裂，形成树冠状的火花。

经蔚县人民政府推荐，该技艺已被列入河北省非物质文化遗产名录，传承人为：薛建国、王德。

“Ladle Tree Flower” is a folk community fire activity originated in the ancient culture of Yu County, Hebei Province. It first appeared in Chenghua Reign of the Ming Dynasty. According to the custom, the performer would use a wet willow spoon soaked in cold water to ladle 1,300°C iron water and splash it on the fortress arch over the gateway. The iron water would crack when it hit the brick wall, and form a crown-shaped fire flower.

Upon recommendation of Yu County People’s Government, the art has been ranked among the Intangible Cultural Heritage of Hebei Province. It’s passed on by Xue Jianguo and Wang De.

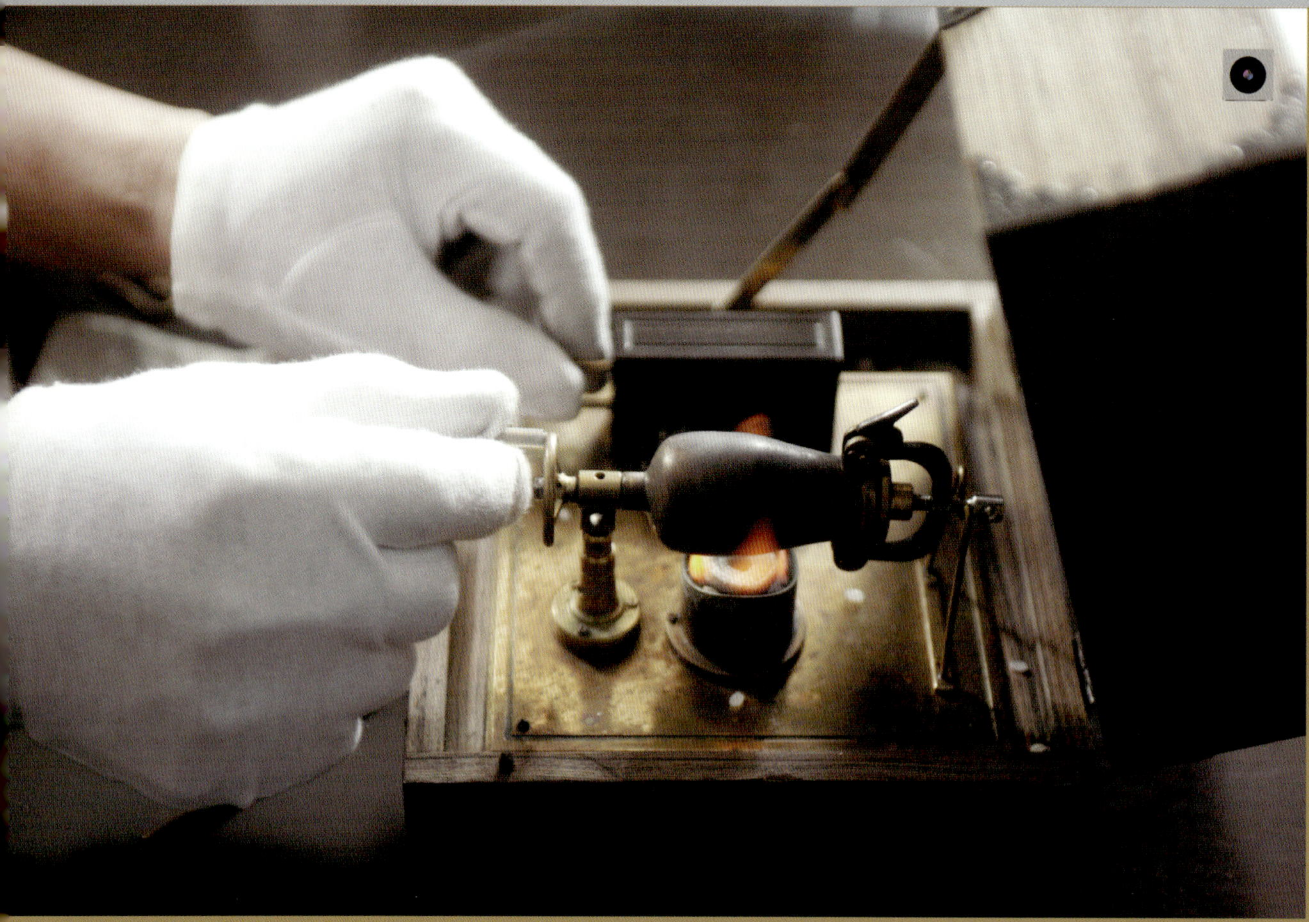

最小的爆米花机

The Smallest Puffed Rice Machine

该爆米花机系手工制作，材质为铜，主机长75毫米，高85毫米，滚筒最大直径32毫米，风箱尺寸64×20×33毫米。用酒精加热，能正常使用。

陆继明（上海）2009年1月7日至2月17日制作完成。

With hand-planted this puffed rice machine was made of copper and the mainframe is 75 millimeters, height is 85 millimeters, most large diameter of the platen is 32 millimeters. The size of the bellows is 64×20×33 millimeter. With the ethyl alcohol heating it can be used normally.

It was made of by Lu Jiming (Shanghai) from January 7, 2009 to February 17.

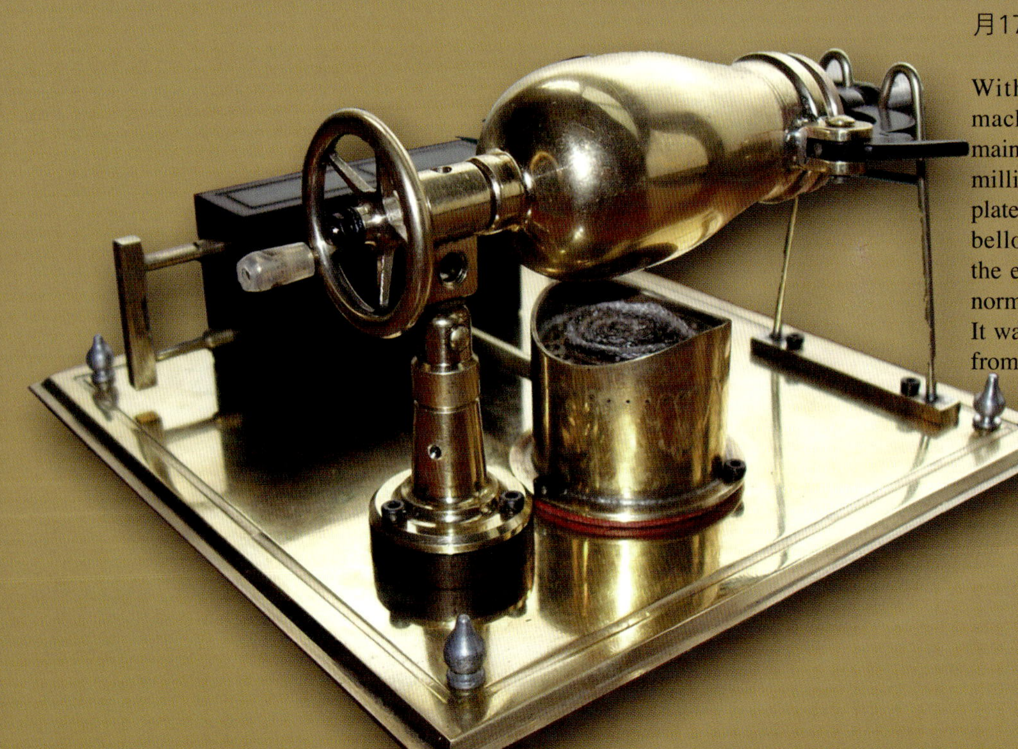

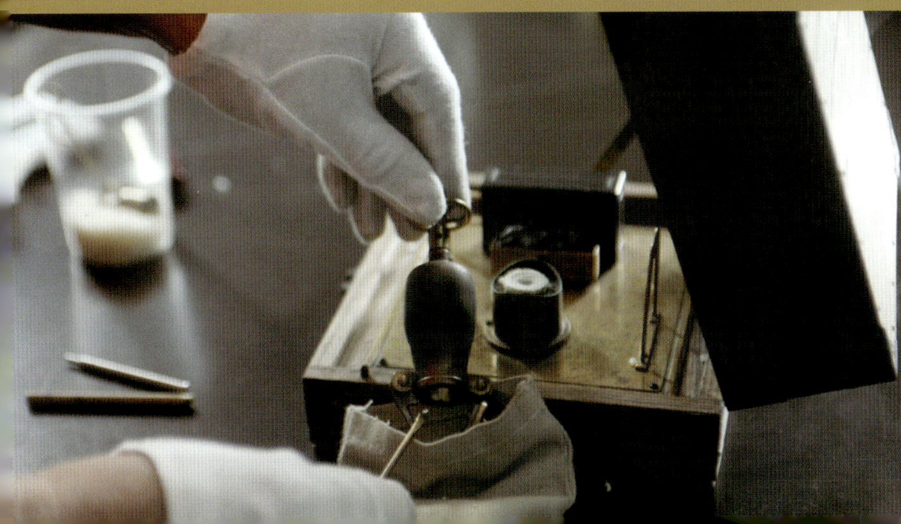

自著、自书**最长**的书法长卷

——《新三字经》

The Longest Calligraphy Volume
– "New 3-Character Primer"

长: **48** 米　高: **0.76** 米

The length: 48 meters
Width: 0.76 meter

《新三字经》由高占祥（北京）著，中国人民大学出版社出版。2008年10月5日高占祥将1416字的《新三字经》书写成长卷。

With 1, 416 character "New 3-character primer" was written by Gao Zhanxiang (Beijing) on Oct 5, 2008 and it was published by Renmin University of China press.

面积**最大**的冷光烟花图案

——中华人民共和国国旗

Biggest Pattern of the Luminescent Fireworks –National Flag of the PRC

2009年5月19日由湖南庆典烟花制造燃放有限公司制作的冷光烟花（中华人民共和国国旗图案）在第九届中国（浏阳）国际花炮节上成功燃放，冷光烟花采用无线程控进行操作，在中华人民共和国国歌声中冉冉升起，总时间为60秒。

The luminescent fireworks titled the National Flag of the PRC made by Hunan Ceremony Fireworks Manufacturing and Lighting Co., Ltd was successfully set off in the 9th China (Liuyang) International Fireworks Festival. It's operated by the wireless control and slowing rise up in the national anthem of the PRC lasting 60 seconds.

尺寸：42×28 米
Size: 42 × 28m

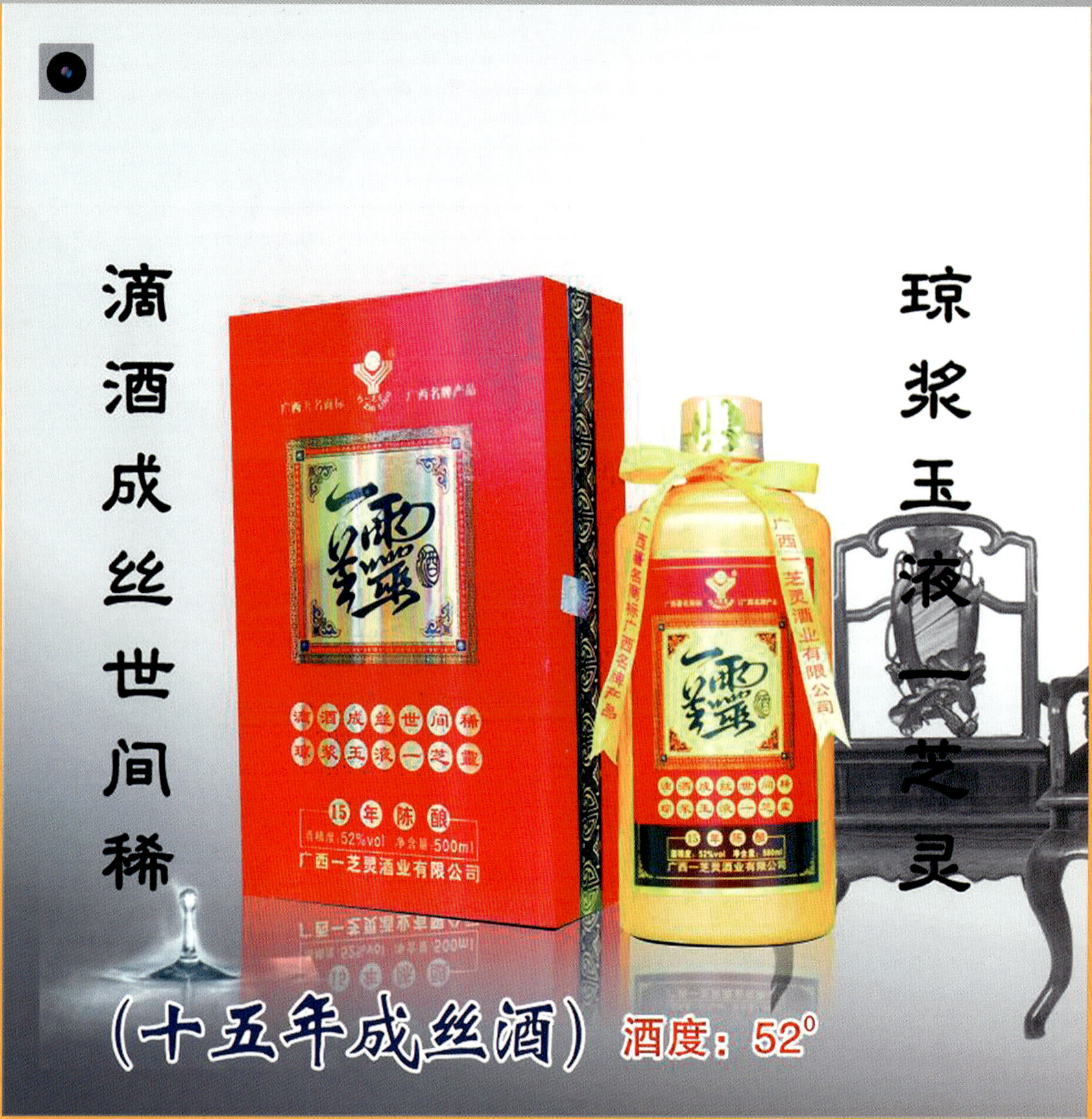
滴酒成丝世间稀
琼浆玉液一芝灵
（十五年成丝酒）
酒度：52°
广西一芝灵酒业有限公司

滴酒成丝高度之最

——“一芝灵玉龙宴酒（52度）”

Highest Threadlike Spirit Drop – Yizhiling Yulongyan (52°)

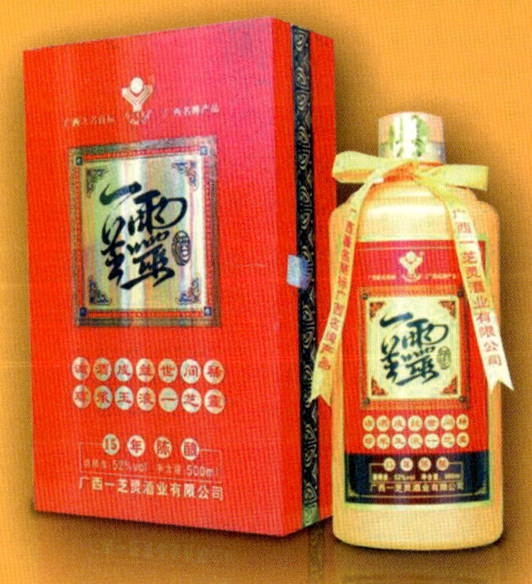

2011年11月2日相关检测部门在广西桂平市一芝灵酒厂样品室，对该厂生产的“一芝灵玉龙宴酒”滴酒成丝进行检测，从2米高斟酒入杯，酒丝连绵不断。

On November 2, 2011, the testing authorities tested the threadlike drop of Yizhiling Yulongyan spirit in the sample room of Yizhiling Distillery in Guiping, Guangxi. The spirit formed threadlike drops when poured into the cup from a place 2m high.

220cm
200cm
高度：2 米
Height: 2m
150cm
100cm
50cm

高度：34 厘米

数量：20 只

Height: 34cm

Number of dices: 20

张经林（河南·夏邑）2006年8月20日在浙江省温州市假日大舞台创造。

Zhang Jinglin (Xiayi Henan) created this record at Holiday Large Stage in Wenzhou, Zhejiang on August 20th 2006.

摇骰子叠高之最（单排）

Folding Dices Highest (a single line)

含最多不重样人物造型的环保软陶作品
——"承上启下"

The Environment-friendly Polymer Clay Works with the Most Different Characters —"Carrying Forward"

该作品高63厘米，最长处110厘米，最宽处89厘米，整体以绿色为基调，100个人物造型形态各异，展现耕作、嬉戏、学习等五个场景。

上海工艺美术厂孙佩、樊黎明（上海）选用环保软陶材料2011年4月至10月手工捏制而成。

63cm in height, 110cm in maximum length and 89cm in maximum width, it has an overall green tone and 100 characters in different shapes showing five scenes, i.e., farming, playing, learning, etc.

It was made of environment-friendly polymer clay between April and October of 2011 by Sun Pei and Fan Liming (Shanghai) from Shanghai Arts & Crafts Factory.

数量:100

Number of characters: 100

最大的根雕作品

——《清明上河图》

The Largest Root Carving Works
– Riverside Scene at Qingming Festival

该作品选用天然香樟树根于2009年6月至2012年3月雕刻，重30吨。

深圳市官道投资股份有限公司收藏。

The works, 30t in weight, was carved from natural Camphor tree root from June, 2009 to March, 2012. Collected by Shenzhen Guandao Investment Co., Ltd.

长：25.002 米　最宽处：2.35 米　最高处：3.03 米

The length: 25.002m; the width: 2.35m; the height: 3.03m

拥有“福建土楼”最多的县

——福建省永定县

the County with the Most “Fujian Tulou” (Earth Building)-Yongding County, Fujian Province

该县现存“福建土楼”23000座，遍布各个乡镇、村落，其中圈数最多、建筑规模最大的为“承启楼”；最高的为“永隆昌楼”；最古老的为“龙安寨”（始建于唐朝）。永定县人民政府管理。

The county currently possesses a total of 23, 000 Fujian Tulous (earth buildings), which was scattered around the towns and villages of the county. Among the buildings, the one with the most circles and largest scale is “Chengqi Lou”; the tallest is “Yonglongchang Lou”; the most ancient is “Longan Zhai” (Originally built in the Tang Dynasty). The buildings are preserved and administrated by the People’s Government of Yongding County.

数量：23,000座
No. of Tulous: 23, 000

最大的客家梯田
——“江西·崇义上堡梯田”
The Biggest Hakka Terrace
— "Shangbao Terrace of Chongyi, Jiangxi"
面积：1.2 万亩
Area: 12,000 mu

该梯田位于江西省崇义县上堡乡客家地区，开建于南宋时期，客家先民迁徙此地依山建房，开山凿田，耕地面积占全乡94.5%，上百级梯田层层叠叠蜿蜒向上，散落于全乡群山峻岭。

江西省崇义县人民政府管理。

The terrace is located in Hakka regions of Shangbao Village, Chongyi Country, Jiangxi Province. It was initially built in the Southern Song Dynasty. The original residents were Hakkas who immigrated here. They made mountains into fields and built houses nearby, and the cultivated lands account for 94.5% of the entire village. The terrace tiers and winds up in hundreds of levels, scattering among the high mountains and lofty hills in the whole village.

It is managed by the People's Government of Chongyi County of Jiangxi Province.

最大的水拓画

The Smallest Puffed Rice Machine

长：52 米 宽：4.8 米

面积：249.6 平方米

Length 52m Width 4.8m Area 249.6m^2.

秦建良(上海)1993年3月20日在上海辽阳中学创作完成，所用时间10分钟。

Created by Qin Jianliang (Shanghai)in 10 minutes at Liaoyang Middle School in Shanghai on March 20, 1993.

靴底长：2.14 米
靴筒高：3.38 米
总重：410 公斤
Length of sole: 2.14 m
Height of bootleg: 3.38 m
Total weight: 410 kg

最大的蒙古靴
——“巨型鄂尔多斯马海”

The Biggest Mongolian Boot
— Gigantic Ordos Mahai Boot

该蒙古靴选用驴皮12张、羊皮3张、绸绳75公斤、麻绳50公斤、布600米以贴花、缝缀、刺绣等传统蒙古族纯手工艺制作，靴面装饰有花草、鸟兽、犄纹、云纹、狩猎等刺绣图案。

德力格尔玛（内蒙古·鄂尔多斯）2008年5月至2012年7月缝制而成，内蒙古鄂尔多斯市鄂托克旗文化局收藏。

This kind of Mongolian boot is made from selected donkey hide (12 sheets), sheepskin (3 sheets), silk rope (75 kg), hemp rope (50 kg), and cloth (600 m), by appliqué, stitching, embroidering and other traditional Mongolian handicrafts. Its vamp is decorated with embroideries such as flowers and grasses, birds and beasts, horn, cloud, hunting and etc.

De Liglma (Ordos, Inner Mongolia) has stitched and completed it during May, 2008 to July, 2012. It is collected by the Otog Banner Department of Cultural Affairs in Ordos, Mongolia.

篇幅**最多**的单面皮雕书法作品

——《蒙古秘史》

Longest Calligraphic Work Carved in One Side of Leather – Secret History of Mongolia

数量：185块（尺寸：1.2×0.6米/块）
Quantity: 185 pieces
(Size: 1.2×0.6m/piece)

该单面皮雕书法作品将《蒙古秘史》以蒙文形式并采用阴刻技法雕刻，全长111米。
内蒙古鄂托克旗文化广播电影电视局管理，现展于内蒙古鄂尔多斯市成吉思汗陵。

The work was carved in intaglio technique in Mongolian language, 111m long in total.
It's managed by Inner Mongolia Etuoke Banner Culture, Broadcast, Film and TV Bureau. Now it's on display in Genghis Khan Mausoleum, Erdos, Inner Mongolia.

最长的电子版动态画
——《清明上河图》

尺寸：128×6.5米
Size: 128 × 6.5 m

Longest Electronic Version of Dynamic Painting – "Riverside Scene at Qingming Festival"

本作品以现代多媒体技术重现了北宋张择端的名画《清明上河图》，展现了中国古代城市的昼夜风景。作品时长约4分钟，在中国2010年上海世博会中国国家馆“智慧的长河”展区循环播放。

本作品由上海世博会事务协调局策划并组织创作，由北京水晶石数字科技有限公司上海分公司于2010年4月制作完成。

Famous painting "Riverside Scene at Qingming Festival" drawn by Zhang Zeduan in the Northern Song Dynasty was reproduced with modern multimedia technology, showing the scenery of ancient Chinese city day and night. The scene lasts about 4 minutes and it was repeatedly played at "Wisdom of Long River" exhibition area in China Pavilion during 2010 Shanghai World Expo.

This work was planned and organized by the Bureau of Shanghai World Expo Coordination, and made by Shanghai Branch of Beijing Crystal Digital Technology Co., Ltd. in April, 2010.

数量：50 把
Quantity: 50 bundle

徒手速拧钢勺数量之最（一分钟）

The largest number of speed twisting steel ladle unarmed (in one minute)

张诗伟（北京）一分钟内将50把钢勺（长19厘米，勺柄最细处周长14毫米）拧成麻花状，勺柄旋转≥180°。

2013年7月22日在上海市淮海中路1号柳林大厦创造。

Zhang Shiwei(Beijing) twisted 50 bundle of steel ladle (the length is 19cm and the finest point of its handle is 14mm) into braid in one minute and the ladle's handle rotated greater than equal to 180°.

It is created in the Liulin Building that located in No.1, Middle Huaihai Road, Shanghai on July 22, 2013.

人工养殖大雁放飞数量之最

Maximum Artificial Breeding Wild Geese Flying

数量：15450 只

Quantity: 15,450 wild geese

崔本君（吉林·白城）自2006年9月至今在吉林省通榆县向海乡鹤乡大雁养殖场像家鸽一样放养大雁，每天早晨飞出雁舍到附近的草原和泡泽觅食，傍晚归巢。

Cui Benjun (from White City, Jilin) bred a large number of wild geese at the Hexiang Wild Goose Breeding Farm of Xianghai Township in Tongyu County, Jilin Province, since September, 2006. The wild geese would fly out of the nests, in the way similar to pigeon, to nearby grassland and pond for food, and return to their nests every evening.

规模最大的单日自行车骑游活动（异地出发）

——“锦州市喜迎世园会文明伴我行 万人骑行 奔世园活动”

The Largest Single-day Bicycle Riding Activity(set out from different places)
– “Jinzhou Celebrating World Landscape Art Exposition & Courtesy Being with me & Thousand People Riding to the WLAE Activity”

数量：10111

Number of attendents: 10,111

2013年5月25日为庆祝“2013中国锦州世界园林博览会”成功举办，辽宁省锦州市公安交通警察支队、共青团渤海大学委员会、锦州市教育局、锦州广播电视台直播锦州栏目组、锦州捷安特自行车运动俱乐部联合组织10111位骑行爱好者从锦州市各地骑至“2013中国锦州世界园林博览会”园区。

On May 25, 2013, to celebrate the successful holding of the “2013 World Landscape Art Exposition Jinzhou China”, the public security and traffic police branch in Jinzhou city, Liaoning province, the Committee of Communist Youth League in Bohai Univerty, the Education Bureau of Jinzhou city, the program group of “Live Broadcast Jinzhou” in Radio & Television Jinzhou and the Jinzhou Giant Bicycle sports club together organized 10,111 cycling fans to ride from all around the Jinzhou city to the exhibition area of “2013 World Landscape Art Exposition Jinzhou China”

面积最大的水上芦荡迷宫
——"盐城大纵湖水上芦荡迷宫"

Largest Reed Marshes Maze
– Yancheng Dazhong Lake Reed Marshes Maze

面积：140905 平方米
水面面积：70169 平方米
芦苇面积：70736 平方米
Total area: 140,905m^2
Area of water: 70,169m^2
Area of reed: 70,736m^2

“盐城大纵湖水上芦荡迷宫”位于盐城大纵湖旅游度假区内，迷宫内有三条主航道，平均水深约1米，总长度约7650米（其中1号主航道长约500米，平均宽度约12米；2号主航道长约900米，平均宽度约15米；3号主航道长约1100米，平均宽度约15米）。

盐城大纵湖水上芦荡迷宫于2004年3月6日至5月8日建成。

Dazong Lake Reed Marshes Maze is situated at resort area of Dazong lake in Yancheng of Jiangsu Province. There are three main waterways in it. The average water depth is about 900 meters and the total length is 7,650 meters (The first main waterway is about 500 meters long and 12 meters wide on the average: the second is about 900 meters long and 15 meters wide on the average; the third is about 1,100 meters long and 15 meters wide on the average).

The maze project was built from March 6 to May 8 in 2004.

最大的石榴园林 ——“冠世榴园”

Largest Megranate Garden – “Champion of Megranate Garden”

种植面积:10万亩 品种:43种
数量:500万株 年总产量:2250万公斤
Planting Area: 6,670 hectares
Varieties: 43 Numbers: 5,000,000
Annual total output: 22,500,000kg

国中国
一望亭
青檀寺
三近书院
匡衡墓

该石榴园林位于山东省枣庄市峄城区境内，东西长45华里、南北宽6华里，开辟培植至今已有2000余年，其中石榴的花色有红、白、黄、橙等多种，山东省枣庄市峄城区人民政府管理。

With a long history of cultivation of more than 2,000 years, it is located at Yicheng District, Zaozhuang City, Shandong Province; its longitude from east to west is 45 li while its width from north to south is 6 li. The colors of Megranate are red, white, yellow and orange, etc. Now it is administrated by the Government of Yicheng District, Zaozhuang City, Shandong Province.

该木化石（硅化木）发掘于广西，呈完整树形状，有树根、树干、树叶三部分组成。

沈德全（澳门）、黄威廉（澳门）1991年8月收藏。

This wood fossil (silicified wood), which was excavated in Guangxi Province, has a shape of an intact tree. The fossil consists of three parts: roots, trunk and leaves. Dequan Shen (Macau) and William Huang (Macau) took the fossil into their collection in Aug, 1991.

最大的完整树形木化石

The Biggest Intact Tree-shape Wood Fossil

最高处：1.8 米 最宽处：1.6 米
重：2.2 吨
The Highest Section: 1.8m
The Broadest Section: 1.6m
Weight: 2.2 ton.

最大的翡翠雕刻作品 ——翠“寿”佛

The Biggest Emerald Sculpture —Emerald "Longevity" Buddha

该作品材质为缅甸密支那些老坑翠玉矿黑砂皮，主体雕像为观世音菩萨，文殊、普贤菩萨立于两旁，周围雕有形态各异的腾龙、苍松、翠柏、楼阁、亭台等，采用立体圆雕、深浅浮雕、镂空透雕等工艺技法经15年雕刻而成。

Lip Ming Kuo（葡萄牙籍华裔）2009年12月收藏。

This piece of sculpture is made of black cortex produced from old emerald mine at Mitkyina in Myanmar. The main statue is the Bodhisattva, flanked by Manjushri and Samantabhadra on both sides. Various shapes of soaring dragons, pines and cypresses, pavilions and kiosks are carved all around. Crafts and techniques, including three-dimensional round carving, depth perceptional bas-relief, hollow carving and perspective engraving have been adopted for the completion of this sculpture, which being carved for 15 years.

Lip Ming Kuo (Portuguese citizen of Chinese origin) collected it in December 2009.

重:31.8吨 高:4.6米 宽3.9米 厚:2米

Weight: 31.8 ton Height: 4.6 m;

Wide: 3.9 m; Thick: 2 m.

最大的砺金唐卡

Largest Gilding Tangka

画芯尺寸：2.51×1.39 米
装裱：3.81×1.5 米
Core size: 2.51 × 1.39m
Framing: 3.81 × 1.5m

砺金唐卡是将砺金技法融于传统唐卡绘画技法中。

该作品绘有释迦牟尼、文殊菩萨及普贤菩萨等诸佛菩萨画像。

郑希林（北京）创作，2011年3月31日装裱完成。

Gilding Tangka integrates the gilding technique into the traditional Tangka painting technique.

It has depicted the portraits of many Bodhisattvas, including Sakyamuni, Manjusri and Samantabhadra.

It was created by Zheng Xilin (from Beijing) and the framing was completed on March 31, 2011.

最大的金丝楠木佛像　——“阿弥陀佛”

Amitabha – The Largest Buddha Statue Made of Phoebe Zhennan

佛像高：5.8 米

Height of Buddha Statue: 5.8m

该佛像系马云峰（北京）选用金丝楠木雕刻，由佛像、背光、莲花座、须弥底座等组成，总高13米。2006年1月至2008年8月完工，现供奉于北京市天宁寺。

This Buddha statue is carved by Ma Yunfeng (Beijing) with selected Phoebe Zhennan. Counting all parts in, including Buddha statue, backlight, lotus throne and Meru pedestal, the total height is 13m.
The creation of this statue was started in January 2006 and finished in August 2008. Now, it is enshrined in Tianning Temple, Beijing.

最长的玻璃雕刻屏风

The Longest Glass-engraving Screen

长：40.46 米　高：2.53 米

Length: 40.46 M; Height: 2.53 M

该屏风由28块（2.53×1.445米）玻璃链接而成，刻有前言、齐、梁两朝二十六位皇帝肖像及作者自刻像（前言、二十六位皇帝肖像、落款为阴刻，作者自刻像、落款为阳刻，共1502字）。

汤友常（江苏·常州）2009年8月1日至2010年2月11日雕刻完成。

The screen was made of 28 pieces of glass, sized 2.53 × 1.445 meters, and engraved with the preface, and engraved portraits of 26 emperors in the Qi and Liang dynasties, as well as the engraved portrait of the engraver (the preface, 26 portraits of the emperors, and the inscription are in intaglio, while the portrait of the engraver and the inscription are in positive scribing, and there are a total of 1502 words in all).

Tang Youchang (from Changzhou, Jiangsu) started engraving on August 1, 2009 and completed the work on February 11, 2010.

最大的独幅成瓷雕刻作品
——“瓷趣”

The Biggest Single Porcelain Sculpture - “Porcelain Fun”

尺寸: 259×130×0.8 厘米
Size: 259 × 130 × 0.8cm

2013年6月14日至7月14日汤友常（江苏·常州）使用切割刀在独幅瓷板上阴刻荷花、荷叶、河虾、螃蟹、蜻蜓、小鸟等图案并落款45字及篆书姓氏印章1枚。

From June 14 to July 14 of 2013, Tang Youchang(Jiangsu·Changzhou) used cutting knife to intaglio pictures like lotus, lotus leaf, shrimp, crab, dragonfly and bird in the single porcelain plate. He also inscribed 45 characters on it and scripted one surname seal.

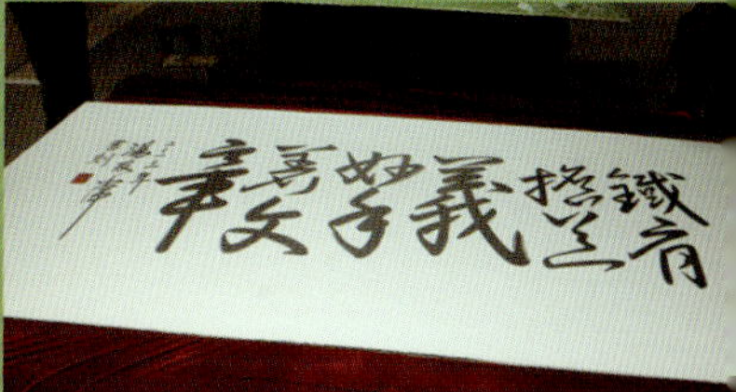

单人抽动陀螺重量之最（女）

Single Twitching of Top with the Weight of the Most(female)

重：176.5 公斤　高：27.5 厘米　直径：37 厘米

Weight: 176.5kg　Height: 27.5cm　Diameter: 37cm

汤留凤（江苏·常州）抽打该陀螺，使其持续转动1分53秒。

2013年6月10日在江苏省常州市新北区孟河镇孟河大道18号龙凤楼内“汤友常文化展示中心”独自完成。

Tang Liufeng(Jiangsu·Changzhou) twitched that top and kept it moving for 1 minute and 53 seconds.

On June 10,2013, it was completed in the “Tang Youchang Culture Exhibition Center” that located in Longfeng Building in the 18th Menghe Avenue , Menghe county , Changzhou city, Jiangsu province.

单人抽动陀螺重量之最（少年）

Single Twitching of Top with the Weight of the Most (junior)

重：150.5 公斤　高：23.5 厘米　直径：37 厘米

Weight: 150.5kg Height: 23.5cm Diameter: 37cm

薛天禧（江苏·常州）抽打该陀螺，使其持续转动1分36秒。

2013年6月10日在江苏省常州市新北区孟河镇孟河大道18号龙凤楼内“汤友常文化展示中心”独自完成。

Xue Tianxi(Jiangsu·Changzhou) twitched that top and kept it moving for 1 minute and 36 seconds.

On June 10, 2013, it was completed alone in the “Tang Youchang Culture Exhibition Center” that located in Longfeng Building in the 18th Menghe Avenue , Menghe county , Changzhou city, Jiangsu province.

规模最大的传世铜鼓展演活动

Oldest "Ladle Tree Flower" Folklore

数量：500

Number of performers: 500

2011年12月10日“河池第十二届铜鼓山歌艺术节”在广西河池市文化广场举行，现场由东兰县人民政府组织500位表演者使用民间传世的铜鼓（鼓面直径27–55厘米不等）进行大型铜鼓展演活动。

On December 10, 2011, the 12th Hechi Bronze Drum & Folk Song Arts Festival was held in the Cultural Square in Hechi, Guangxi Province. 500 performers were organized by the Government of Dongshan County to play the ancient bronze drums (the diameters of drums are from 27 to 55 cm).

重:269.4公斤
Weight: 269.4KG

最重的瘿木瘤作品 ——“万花聚瘿”

Heaviest Work of Tree Knag – Flower Knag

“万花聚瘿”选用杉木根生瘿木瘤，按其原型加工，制作成直径1.5米，周长4.7米的圆桌。
唐祥元（江苏·常熟）1992年2月6日收藏。

It was made of a knag of a fir root according to its original shape and made into a round table with a diameter of 1.5m and perimeter of 4.7m. It was collected by Tang Xiangyuan (Changshu, Jiangsu) on

图书在版编目（CIP）数据

2013大世界基尼斯纪录画册：互动版 / 上海大世界基尼斯总部编. -- 上海：文汇出版社, 2014.2

ISBN 978-7-5496-0857-7

Ⅰ. ①2　Ⅱ. ①上　Ⅲ. ①科学知识—普及读物
Ⅳ. ①Z228

中国版本图书馆CIP数据核字(2014)第002646号

大世界基尼斯纪录画册（互动版）

上海大世界基尼斯总部　编

责任编辑 / 卫　中
装帧设计 / 陈益平

出版发行 / 文匯出版社

地址：上海威海路755号（邮编：200041）

经　　销 / 全国新华书店
印刷装订 / 上海锦佳印刷有限公司
版　　次 / 2014年2月第1版
印　　次 / 2014年2月第1次印刷
开　　本 / 889×1194　1/16
字　　数 / 150千
印　　张 / 7.5
书　　号 / ISBN 978-7-5496-0857-7
定　　价 / 200.00元